TOOLS FOR TEACHERS

- **ATOS:** 0.5
- **GRL:** C
- **WORD COUNT:** 29

- **CURRICULUM CONNECTIONS:**
  nature, seeds, trees

Skills to Teach

- **HIGH-FREQUENCY WORDS:** a, is, it, makes, the
- **CONTENT WORDS:** falls, grows, inside, nut, root, seed, tree
- **PUNCTUATION:** periods, exclamation point
- **WORD STUDY:** long /o/, spelled *ow* (*grows*); long /e/, spelled *ee* (*seed*, *tree*); initial consonant blends (*grows*, *tree*)
- **TEXT TYPE:** factual description

Before Reading Activities

- Read the title and give a simple statement of the main idea.
- Have students "walk" though the book and talk about what they see in the pictures.
- Introduce new vocabulary by having students predict the first letter and locate the word in the text.
- Discuss any unfamiliar concepts that are in the text.

After Reading Activities

In the story, a tree grows a seed that in time becomes another tree. Invite readers to discuss what they think needs to happen to seeds in order for them to become plants or trees. Prompt them by asking, "Do seeds need water to grow? Do seeds need sunlight to grow?" Write their answers on the board and discuss.

Reader

Tadpole Books are published by Jump!, 5357 Penn Avenue South, Minneapolis, MN 55419, www.jumplibrary.com

Copyright ©2018 Jump. International copyright reserved in all countries. No part of this book may be reproduced in any form without written permission from the publisher.

Editorial: Hundred Acre Words, LLC   **Designer:** Anna Peterson

Photo Credits: Alamy: MShieldsPhotos, 4–5. Getty: Davies and Starr, cover. Shutterstock: Billion Photos, 10–11; Golden Brown, 6–7; Madlen, 8–9; Marythepooh, 2–3; Oksana Samorodnaia, 14–15; visuall2, 12–13; Volodymyr Tsyba, 1.

Library of Congress Cataloging-in-Publication Data
Names: Mayerling, Tim, author.
Title: I see seeds/ by Tim Mayerling.
Description: Minneapolis, Minnesota: Jump!, Inc., 2017. | Series: Outdoor explorer | Audience: Age 3–6. | Includes index.
Identifiers: LCCN 2017045156 (print) | LCCN 2017044084 (ebook) | ISBN 9781624967306 (ebook) | ISBN 9781620319635 (hardcover: alk. paper) | ISBN 9781620319642 (paperback: alk. paper)
Subjects: LCSH: Seeds—Juvenile literature.
Classification: LCC QK661 (print) | LCC QK661 .M39 2017 (ebook) | DDC 581.4/67—dc23
LC record available at https://lccn.loc.gov/2017045156

OUTDOOR EXPLORER

I SEE SEEDS

by Tim Mayerling

TABLE OF CONTENTS

tadpole
books

I SEE SEEDS

nut

A tree makes a nut.

seed

Inside is a seed.

The seed falls.

root

It takes root.

It grows.

It becomes a tree.

13

The tree makes a seed!

WORDS TO KNOW

falls

grows

nut

root

seed

tree

INDEX